CONFIDENTIAL

MINISTRY OF HOME SECURITY

OBJECTS DROPPED
FROM THE AIR

1941

The Naval & Military Press Ltd

Published by

The Naval & Military Press Ltd
Unit 5 Riverside, Brambleside
Bellbrook Industrial Estate
Uckfield, East Sussex
TN22 1QQ England

Tel: +44 (0)1825 749494

www.naval-military-press.com
www.nmarchive.com

In reprinting in facsimile from the original, any imperfections are inevitably reproduced and the quality may fall short of modern type and cartographic standards.

OBJECTS DROPPED FROM THE AIR.

This handbook is intended to help in the identification of objects dropped from the air.

Until the harmless nature of any object is established, it should be approached with care and all the precautions laid down should be strictly observed. The public should, in all cases, be prevented from handling objects which are suspected of being dropped from aircraft.

Among the objects which may be found on the ground dropped from the air are :—

1. German high explosive and incendiary bombs (p. 2).
2. Italian high explosive and incendiary bombs (p. 6).
3. Parachute mines (p. 7)
4. Aircraft demolition bombs (p. 8).
5. German small arms ammunition (p. 8).
6. German machine-gun magazines (p. 10).
7. German incendiary bomb containers (p. 10).
8. Message tubes (p. 13).
9. Whistle attachments for screaming bombs (p. 13).
10. Auxiliary plywood petrol tanks (p. 14).
11. Wireless apparatus (p. 14).
12. Flares and flare parachutes (p. 14).
13. Dye-bags (p. 16).
14. Meteorological balloons (p. 16).
15. Leaflet - carrying balloons (p. 17).
16. Leaflet-carrying parachutes (p. 18).
17. Man-carrying parachutes (p. 18).
18. British practice bombs (p. 19).
19. British smoke floats (p. 19).

The following descriptions and illustrations (shown on pages enumerated above) will facilitate the recognition of these objects, which should be disposed of in accordance with existing instructions for the disposal of unexploded bombs and parachute mines and, as regards other objects, through the agency of the Police, in accordance with the instructions they have received.

1. German Bombs.

(a) High Explosive Bombs.

The range of the known types of German high explosive bombs is shown in Figure 1 and the accompanying Table A which gives their principal dimensions. Fragments of these bombs, and particularly of the tail pieces, are frequently found near the scene of an explosion, and it may be possible in some cases to identify them from the particulars given here.

TABLE A

GERMAN H.E. BOMBS

1. *General Purpose Bombs*

Weight	Approx. overall length	Length of body without vanes	Max. diam. body	Approx. H.E. charge	Approx. wall thickness main body	Approx. thickness of nose piece from tip to main body	German Name
	ft. in.	ft. in.	in.		in.	in.	
50 kg. (110 lb.)	3 6	2 4½	8	24.4 kg.	5/32	1½ to ⅜	
100 kg. (220 lb.)	4 3	2 9	10	50 kg.	5/32	1½ to ⅜	
250 kg. (550 lb.)	5 4	3 11	14½	MKI.130kg. MKII.110kg	MKI. ¼ MKII5 /16	MKI.1½to⅜ MKII.3to½	
500 kg. (1100 lb.)	6 10½	4 9	18½	250 kg.	9/32		
1000 kg. (2200 lb.)	9 1½	6 3	26	450 kg.	9/32—½	5¼ to ¾	'Hermann'
1800 kg. (4000 lb.)	13 3	8 11	26	800 kg.	⅜	5¼ to ¾	'Satan'

2. *Semi Armour-Piercing and Armour-Piercing Bombs.*

Weight		Approx. overall length	Length of body without vanes	Max. diam. body	Approx. H.E. charge	Approx. wall thickness from tip of nose to main body	German Name
		ft. in.	ft. in.	in.		in.	
50 kg. (110 lb.)		3 3	1 11½	8	16¼ kg.	1⅜ to ½	
500 kg. (1100 lb.)	Type 1	6 6	4 6	15½	150 kg.	9⅜ to 9/10	
	Type 2	—	3 6½	15½	100 kg.	9¼ to 1½	
1000 kg. (2200 lb.)		7 1½	4 9¾	19¾	210 kg.	14¾ to 1½	"Esau"
1400 kg. (3100lb.)		9 0	6 3	22	300 kg.	12½ to 1¼	"Fritz"

3. *Anti-personnel bombs.*

Weight	Overall length	Max. diam.	Approx. H.E. charge	Approx. wall thickness	Description
	ft. in.	in.		in.	
4 lb.	3½	3¼		⅜	The outer casing—coloured dark grey-green—is a cylinder of sheet metal in two halves which open to form a species of parachute as the bomb falls. The ends of the cylinder become vanes at the end of a cable 5 in. long, which rotate and render the fuse live. **The bomb when unexploded is highly sensitive and handling or strong vibration may explode it.**
10 kg. (22 lb.)	2 0	3½	1 kg.	11/32	

(b) *Incendiary Bombs.*

The principal German incendiary bomb so far used against this country has been the 1 kg. magnesium electron bomb with a thermite filling as illustrated in A.R.P. Handbook No. 9. This bomb is the colour of aluminium, with markings both on the side and on the flat nose.

If when found unignited the holes near the nose are covered with insulating tape the detonator in the nose is probably still " live ".

These bombs are sometimes fitted with an explosive charge, contained in a small metal cylinder about 1 in. in diameter and 1¼ in. long, screwed into the tapered or tail end (see Figure 2). This cylinder will be covered by the tail vanes if they are still in position when the bomb is found unignited. Typical markings, as found on both those with and without the explosive charge, are seen in the illustration. The nose markings of the explosive type sometimes include a red " A."

Magnesium electron bombs, when burning on wet ground, may produce a smell of acetylene, which sometimes gives rise to reports that they are a new type containing calcium carbide.

A larger version of this bomb, 4 in. in diameter and 24 in. long, weighing 12 kg., is also believed to be included in the German range, but has not yet been identified in this country. A proportion of these may also contain an explosive charge.

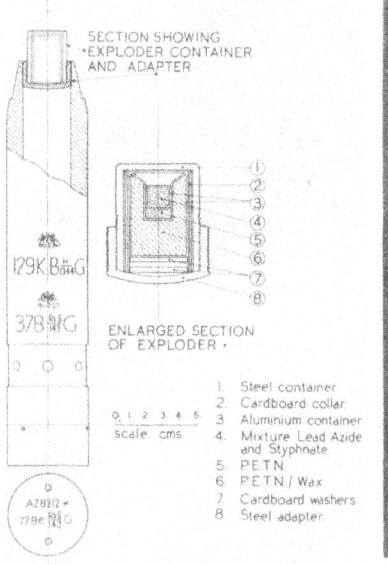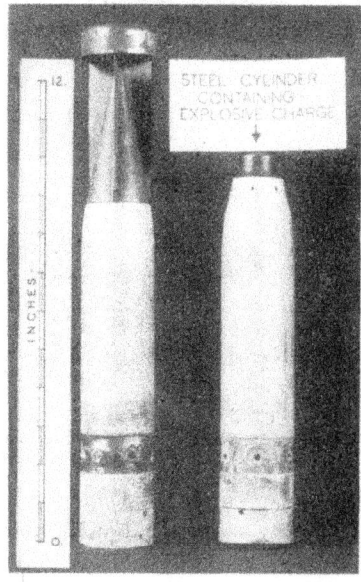

FIGURE 2

There is also an oil bomb, which weighs 110 kg. and has the same external dimensions and to some extent resembles the 250 kg. H.E. bomb. The internal parts of this bomb, which may be scattered after detonation, can be identified from the diagram, Figure 4. The nose piece is usually found intact and is characterised by the aperture seen in Figure 3.

A larger version of this bomb, which has the external dimensions of a 500 kg. H.E. bomb, has also been reported. (N.B. The Germans call these oil bombs *Flammenbomben*, i.e. flame-bombs, one being known as the Flam. 250 and the larger one as Flam. 500.)*

FIGURE 3.

* A few specimens of what at first was thought to be an incendiary bomb, weighing 30 kg., have recently been reported. On examination, they were found, however, to be filled with a flare and not an incendiary composition. This " bomb " has the outer casing of a 50 kg. H.E., but is fitted with a fuse, painted red similar to that used on parachute flares. The following inscription may be found stencilled upon it in black lettering :—

      Lieferungs Nr.
    -   DELEU — Dr. Feistel
      Angefertigt. (Date.).

The casing is spray-painted aluminium and the marking BLC 50 in black letters appears near the tail.

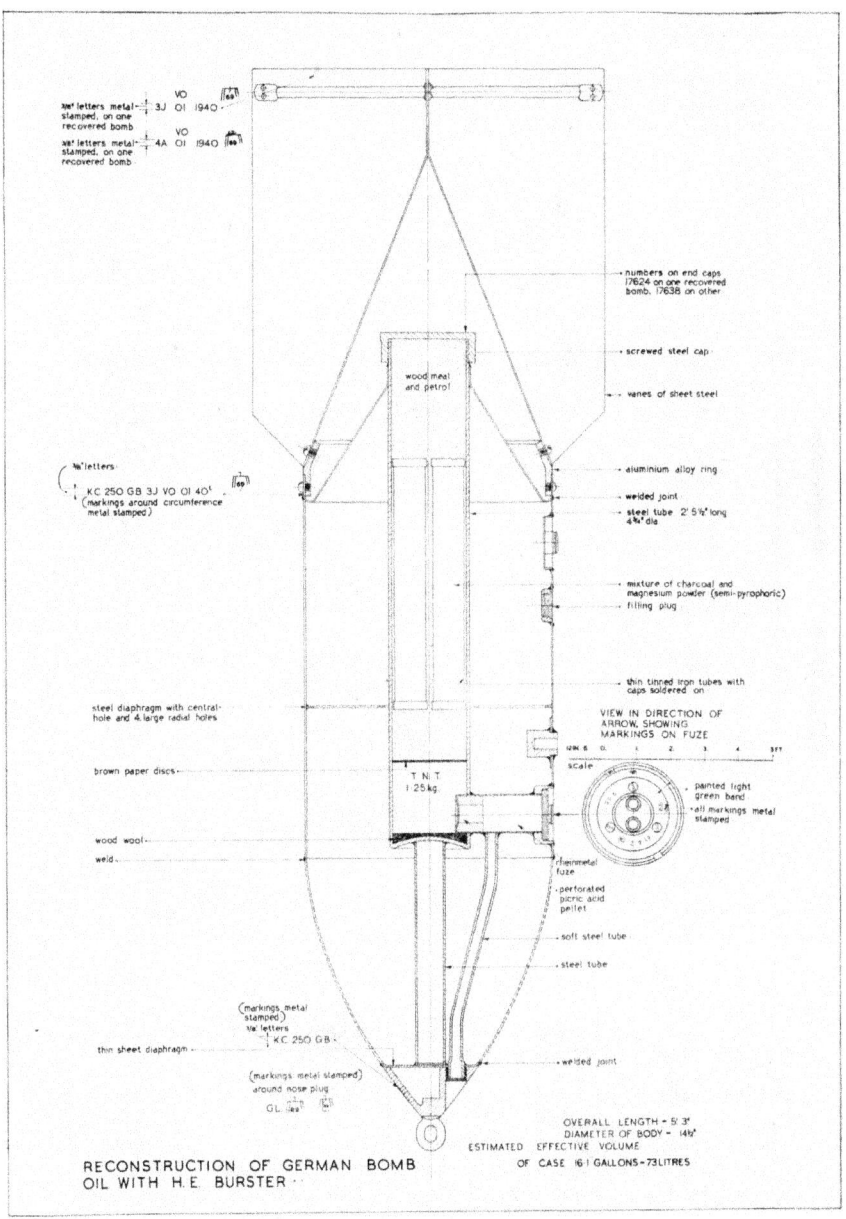

FIGURE 4.

2. Italian Bombs.

The known range of Italian high explosive and incendiary bombs is illustrated in Figure 5 and the accompanying Table B shows the principal dimensions of the H.E. bombs.

TABLE B

ITALIAN H.E. BOMBS

General Purpose.

Weight	Overall Length	Diameter	H.E. Filling
kg.	in.	in.	kg.
50 (110 lb.)	38.5	10	25
100 (220 lb.)	48.5	10	27.5
250 (550 lb.)	79.6	17.8	120
500 (1100 lb.)	101	18	220
800 (1760 lb.)	140	18	357

Anti-Personnel.

2 (4¼ lb.)	5.92	2.75	.36
*4.5 (10 lb.)	13.5	3.5	1
12 (27 lb.)	32.4	3.74	1.8

*This bomb has a sensitive fuse which renders it particularly susceptible to traffic vibration or disturbance.

Italian incendiary bombs are of two types, 2 kg. and 20/25 kg. The former is 10.4 in. long and 2.6 in. in diameter, the body consisting of two cylinders screwed together, one at the nose end containing magnesium and mercuric oxide powder with a small fuse and the rear portion contaning nitro-benzene. This bomb has no tail vanes.

The larger type is about 35 in. long and 6 in. in diameter and is made in three parts joined together by screws.

3. Parachute Mines.

Parachute mines dropped on land in this country so far have been of two types Figures 6 and 7 show the smaller, or " D " type, and Figure 8 the larger, or " C " type. Both types are cylindrical and 2 ft. 2 in. in diameter, the difference being only in the length, which in one is 6 ft. and the other 8 ft. 6 in., without the tail bowl.

The nose of the mine is roughly hemispherical and the other end is hollow, but until released from the aircraft is covered by a hemispherical bowl about 16 in. deep, with the parachute stowed inside. When the mine is dropped from the aircraft, this bowl is pulled off and opens the parachute, to which it is attached by four guy ropes. The bowl may still be attached when it reaches the ground, or may be found some distance away.

FIGURE 6.

FIGURE 7.

FIGURE 8.

The parachute is usually of mixed green and white artificial silk, which gives the whole a sea-green appearance. It is some 27 ft. in diameter, has thick silk cords and allows the mine to fall at about forty miles per hour.

In order to distinguish mines from bombs, it is useful to remember that :—

- (a) Bombs are fitted with vanes ; mines are not.
- (b) Mines have 3 or 4 lugs on the body.
- (c) No object under 5 ft. long is likely to be a mine.
- (d) The rear end of a mine when it reaches the ground is likely to be open.

4. Aircraft-demolition Bombs.

A metal canister, measuring approximately 9 in. by 7 in. by 3 in. and painted German field-grey, is carried in German aircraft. It is intended for the use of the crew in destroying the aircraft should it be forced to land in a hostile country. The canister weighs about 3 kg. and contains T.N.T. In the event of aircraft crashing, these canisters may be thrown some distance from the wreckage, **and should not be tampered with.**

There is a small wire half-loop handle counter-sunk into the top of the canister. Three coloured labels are stuck over holes in the sides ; one being generally fixed at the top near the handle, one in one of the broad sides of the canister, and the third at the bottom. The figure " 3 kg." is also painted in white on one side, and the labels may bear some such inscription in bright orange lettering as :—

Geballte Ladung.   3 kg.   F.P. O2 Sulfiltri ESG.   1938.   RDF. 5 Lief.   1938.

5. German Small Arms Ammunition.

German small arms ammunition is mainly of three calibres, viz. :—

7.92 mm. (0.312 in.), Mauser pattern.

20 mm. (0.8 in.), Oerlikon or Solothurn patterns.

30 mm. (1.2 in.), Solothurn pattern.

Of these, the calibres in commonest use are the 7.92 mm. and 20 mm. In addition, calibres of 13.2 mm. and 15 mm. are known to exist, but so far have been little used.

Each calibre is divided into several types, e.g. ball, armour-piercing, tracer, incendiary—with combinations of armour-piercing and tracer, or armour-piercing and incendiary.

A sketch of a 20 mm. cannon shell is given in Figure 9, and the distinctive features of this and the other types of small arms ammunition are indicated in the accompanying Table C.

Ammunition must not be tampered with in any way, whether it is complete with cartridge case or not. All types are potentially dangerous and some types are particularly so if damaged or if recovered after being fired, as they are then liable to function with the slightest shock.

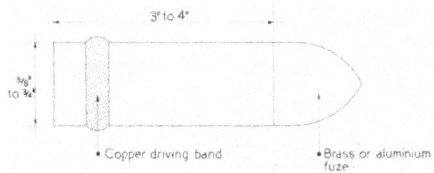

FIGURE 9.

TABLE C
TYPES OF GERMAN SMALL ARMS AMMUNITION.

Item	Calibre mm.	in.	Pattern	Type†	Description	Colour of bullet or other characteristics *
1.	7.92	0.312	Mauser	Ball	Coated steel envelope.	Gilding metal.
2.	,,	,,	,,	A.P.	Coated steel envelope.	Do.
3.	,,	,,	,,	A.P. tracer	Coated steel envelope.	Gilding metal with black tip.
4.	,,	,,	,,	A.P. incendiary (d)	Coated steel envelope.	Gilding metal. The cap of the cartridge case is painted red or has a red or black ring round it.
5.	,,	,,	,,	Incendiary (d)	Percussion fuse; coated steel envelope.	Gilding metal with chromium-plated tip or black with plain gilding metal tip.
6.	20	0.8	Oerlikon	H.E.s.d.t.s. (d)	Shell with various types of sensitive fuse.	Yellow or plain steel, with or without black band or bands. Brass fuse.
7.	,,	,,	,,	Ball	Hollow steel shot.	Olive green.
8.	,,	,,	,,	Ball tracer	Same type of shell body as No. 6, but with inert cap instead of fuse and no H.E. Two similar types.	Olive green with various coloured bands.
9.	,,	,,	,,	H.E. (d)	Solid drawn steel body with round base. Nose fuse. High H.E. capacity.	Yellow with black band below fuse.
10.	20	0.8	Solothurn	A.P. tracer	Pointed steel shell.	Black with yellow band above driving band.
11.	,,	,,	,,	H.E.s.d.t.s. (d)	Similar to Oerlikon pattern (see Item 6 above), with aluminium fuse.	Yellow.
12.	30	1.2	Solothurn	A.P. tracer shell (d)	Pointed steel shell. H.E. with fuse.	Black with yellow band round middle and grey band above driving band.
13.	,,	,,	,,	H.E. tracer (d)	Drawn steel shell; nose fuse.	Yellow with bright aluminium fuse.
14.	13.2	0.52	Solothurn	Tracer		Olive green with white band.
15.	,,	,,	,,	H.E. tracer shell		Yellow.
16.	,,	,,	,,	H.E. incendiary tracer		Yellow with blue band.
17.	15	0.59	,,	Self-destroying tracer shell	Rimless type cartridge, brass cap.	Yellow shell and brass nose fuse, copper driving band.
18.	,,	,,	,,	A.P. tracer	Do.	Black shell and brass nose fuse. Copper driving band.

* Throughout the whole range cartridge cases are normally of brass, but occasionally of steel.

†Types marked (d) are particularly dangerous if they are damaged or if recovered after they have been fired.

A.P.—Armour-piecing. H.E.s.d.t.s.—High explosive self-destroying tracer shell.

6. German Machine-gun Magazines.

The standard German machine-gun magazine of the spectacle type is illustrated in Figure 10. It is about 10 in. long, 4½ in. high and usually has a handle, as shown in the illustration. **It carries about 75 rounds of miscellaneous ammuniton which should be carefully handled.**

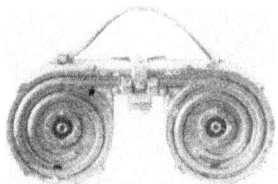

FIGURE 10.

7. Incendiary Bomb Containers.

Four types of container have so far been used by the German Air Force for releasing incendiary bombs of the 1-kg. pattern. These devices, which are frequently, but erroneously, referred to as " Molotoff breadbaskets,"[*] are :—

(a) A rod with brackets.

(b) A cylinder in three side pieces.

(c) A cylinder in two side pieces.

(d) A rectangular canister.

Type (a) carries about 24; types (b) and (c) each 36, and type (d) 15 bombs.

Type (a) is a vertical rod, 43 in. long, with a lug at the top end ; it carries three trays with felt pads, on which the incendiary bombs are stacked vertically round the rod (see Figure 11).

Type (b) is shown in Figure 12. It is composed of three side pieces and a separate end piece, which together form the cylinder illustrated. A clockwork release mechanism, carried on the side near one end (see Figure 12a) has the following German inscription :—

> Achtung ! (Note !)
>
> Verzogerungswerk
>
> aufziehen (Wind up retarding mechanism.)

There is usually a lug for attachment to the bomb carrier, either at the end or, as is shown in the illustration, just above the release mechanism. The container is painted German grey-green or black and is almost always found in three pieces after having released its load. It is approximately 42 in. in length.

[*] The term was applied to a device, used by the Russians in Finland, which contained some 200 small incendiary bombs, scattering them by a rotary action as it fell.

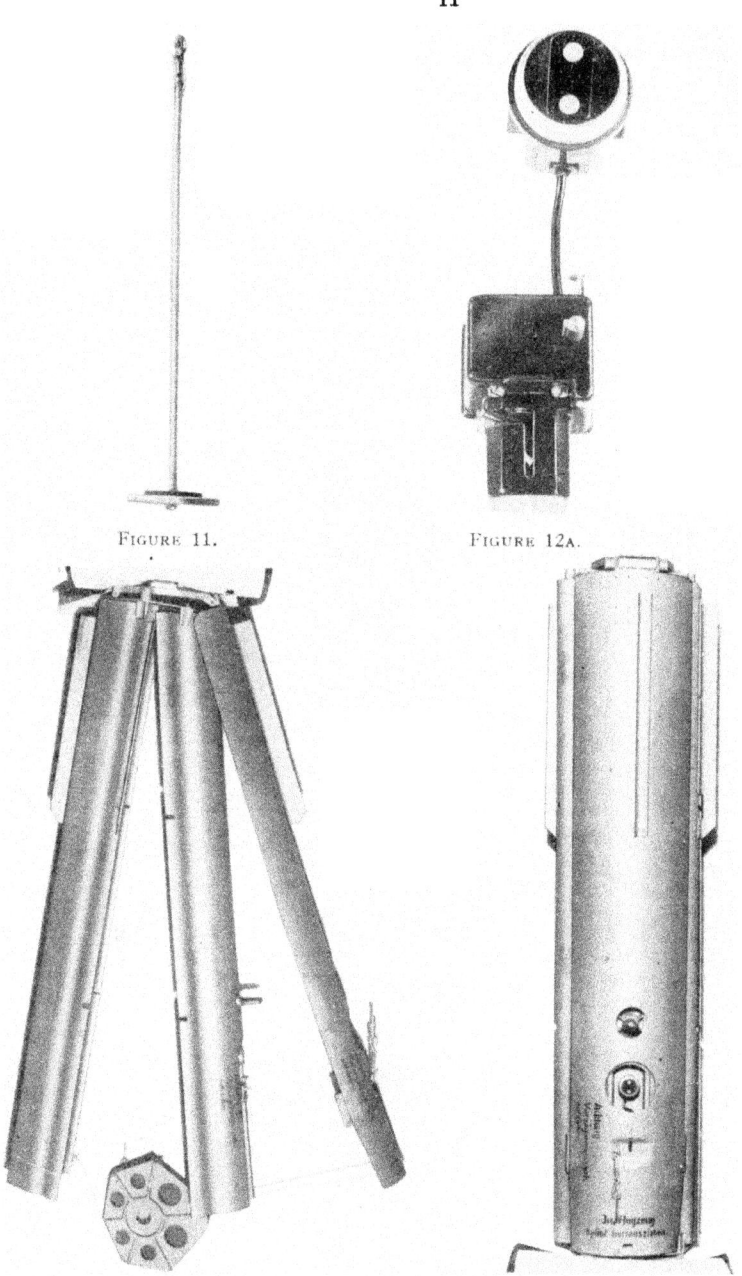

FIGURE 11. FIGURE 12A.

FIGURE 12.

Type (c) (see Figure 13) is a cylinder of two side pieces, with the bottom plate hinged in the middle. Markings on the side of the cylinder are often the letters " A.B.", followed by the number " 36 " in white, the letters " a.s.f." also in white, followed by small black letters on a white ground with a bracket round them, but these markings are likely to be varied. The device is usually painted a dark green. The opening device may be similar to that in Type (b) or may comprise an electrically fired cartridge with a slow match.

Type (d) is a rectangular metal canister with the vertical edges rounded, about 12 in. by 10 in. by 6 in., to carry 15 of the 1-kg. incendiary bombs stacked vertically on end as indicated by the circular marks in Figure 14. The German label on one such container dropped in this country is shown clearly in Figure 15. The lid is 3 in. deep and has a folding handle and felt lining covered by a label.

FIGURE 15

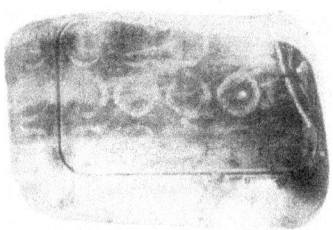

FIGURE 13

FIGURE 14

8. Message Tubes.

A tube used for urgent messages, about 15 in. in length, is shown in Figure 16. It is painted red, with the following German inscription in yellow lettering : Meldebuchse (Land) Fl.24575.

Then follow three German instructions, ending with the words in block letters :—

                UNGEFAHRLICH (not dangerous)
                WICHTIGE MELDUNG ! (important message)
                SOFORT WEITERGEBEN (forward at once)

FIGURE 16

It is opened at one end by a bayonet catch, and is notched at the other end to operate a short delay smoke fuse. These tubes are normally used in Army co-operation duties, but they have been found in this country, usually near crashed enemy aircraft.

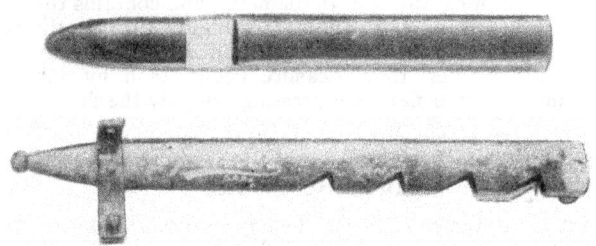

FIGURE 17

9. Whistle Attachments for Screaming Bombs.

Two types of whistle, which are attached to the vanes of German high explosive bombs, causing them to scream as they fall, are illustrated in Figure 17. These whistles are often found near the scene of a bomb explosion.

One type is a black cardboard tube, shaped like an organ pipe. The other model is an adapted bayonet scabbard, with an attachment for fastening it to one of the vanes of the bomb. Both models are approximately 14 in. in length and 1½ in. in diameter, the vent being about 4 in. from the closed end, which is rounded. Owing to mechanical weakness, it often breaks in two at the vent and the parts may be found separately.

In the second type, the body of the pipe is sometimes a hollow sheet-metal tube, spot-welded in two seams down the side, with a wooden nose secured to the tongue of the metal tube by two nails.

(N.B. 1-kg. incendiary bombs have also been found fixed to the vanes of a 50-kg. H.E. bomb by clips.)

10. Auxiliary Plywood Petrol Tanks.

An auxiliary plywood petrol tank, sometimes jettisoned over this country, is illustrated in Figure 18. It is built up from 12-ply wood, glued together. It is torpedo shaped with a tail fin, and has a maximum diameter of 2 ft. 7 in. and an overall length of 11 ft. 6 in.

It is held to the aircraft by a rod with an eyepiece, and is steadied by four stay rods, having ball-joint ends. A vent pipe and rubber suction pipe with a fine mesh strainer made of brass are fitted to the upper side of the tank. The German word *gepruft* (i.e. tested), followed by a date, may be found stencilled on it.

11. Wireless Apparatus.

A form of portable wireless, for use by German airmen who may come down in the sea, is sometimes thrown out of aircraft which break up in the air or crash. This is packed in a sealed metal canister, painted yellow; is 16 in. by 17 in. by 9 in., with handles on the side and German inscriptions on the top.

12. Flares and Flare Parachutes.

Parachute flares are of two main types, one has a single candle, the other has four. The complete unit consists of a cylindrical aluminium casing, 3 ft. 3 in. long and 8 in. in diameter, and contains the parachute, detonator and the candle or candles (see Figure 19). In the case of the single candle, this is 24 in. in length and 7 in. in diameter. Where there are four candles, they measure about 24 in. by 3 in. diameter, and are mounted on a flat steel pressing, roughly the shape of a Maltese cross.

The following markings on the outside casing have been seen :—
DEPYFAG 2.40 Lief. 9.

The outside of the candles has the appearance of polished aluminium and usually bears an inscription indicating the maker and date of manufacture, such, for example, as :—

Ausfuhrung Nicolaus 8/1940 (i.e. Nicolaus Pattern August/1940).

Other makers are :—

Eisfeld : Deleu Dr. Feistel : Berck Holtz : Deutsche Pyrotechnische Fabrik A/G : Sawie : Dr. Schmarr.

When found, some, or all, of the candles are likely to be burnt down to a short stump, and will be attached to the housing of the detonator unit, an aluminium pressing resembling a saucepan 5 in. deep (see Figure 20).

The flare parachute is smaller than that used on the parachute mine, being about 10 ft. in diameter with thin cords, and is usually of silk or artificial silk. It has seven segments. With the heavier type of flare, however, the parachute may be as much as 14 ft. 3 in. in diameter, and may have twelve segments.

The parachutes are usually white and bear the mark " Kurt Peterhansel." A flare parachute, however, has been reported marked " Nicolaus."

AUXILIARY PETROL TANK •
Estimated capacity 200 gallons.
Built up of plywood and glued.
Fitted to release gear for jettisoning.

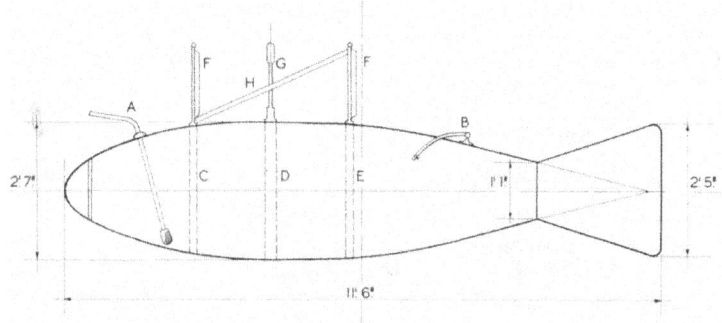

- A   Suction pipe
- B   Vent
- C & E   Circular cross member
- D   Heavy circular cross member and baffle plate
- F   Four steadying rods with ball joint heads
- G   Attachment lug for release
- H   Stay

Not to scale.

FIGURE 18

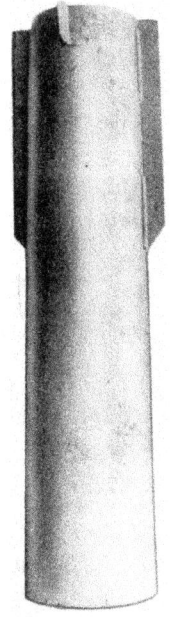

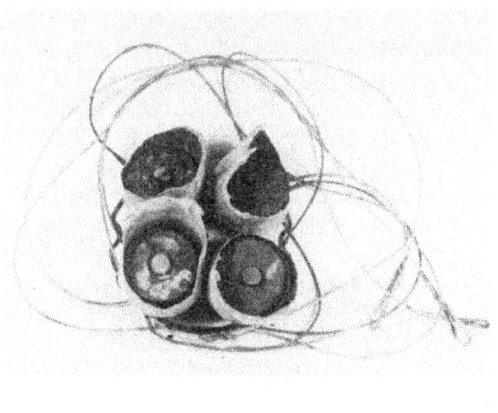

FIGURE 19   FIGURE 20

13. Dye-bags.

Small canvas bags are carried in German aircraft inside a rubberised bag, brown-yellow in colour, about 7½ in. long and about 9½ in. in diameter, which are marked in black letters on the outside with the word " Farbbeutel " (i.e. dye-bag). These bags contain a sodium compound of dye-stuff of the fluorescein type, which is orange-red in colour and is for use in the event of the aircraft falling into the sea. It is very soluble in water and imparts a yellow-red colour to the surrounding sea with intense fluorescence.

14. Meteorological Balloons.

British meteorological balloons comprise :—

(a) A small type about 2 ft. in diameter, many of which have a tail of thread about 25 ft. long with a sheet of coloured paper tied to the end ; they should eventually burst and fall to the ground.

(b) A larger type about 8 ft. in diameter, carrying a meteorograph which, when the balloon bursts, floats down to the ground on a parachute about 3 ft. diameter ; this will usually be found with a label addressed to finder and giving instructions as to its disposal.

Similar devices are used by the Germans and may also be found here. German meteorological balloons are generally made of natural-coloured rubber with a non-fabric strengthener, or are made of latex. They have a peculiar smell which is quite distinct from that of their British counterpart. They can be definitely distinguished, however, by the fact that they are constructed in several segments, whereas, British balloons are all in one piece or in two sections ; or again, by the fact that German balloons have a number of rubber loops cemented on with strings attached to hold the instruments, whereas British balloons have the instruments tied to the neck or valve.

The German balloon measures about 4 ft. long when deflated and weighs from 1 to 2 lb. It often has a small radio transmitter attached, about the size of the box for the general civilian respirator, and also a wire aerial.

All such balloons, both British and German, are liable to leak, in which case they may come to the ground still partially filled with hydrogen.

No naked light or lighted cigarette should be brought too near them, otherwise the gas may ignite, or in the case of larger balloons, cause an explosion.

Apart from the danger of fire, hydrogen is harmless.

15. Leaflet-carrying Balloons.

Two types of German leaflet-carrying balloons have been found so far, one khaki and the other silver, but apart from colour they appear identical. As will be seen from the illustration (Figure 21), they are in the form of a vertical cylinder with rounded ends, and measure when deflated about 16 ft. by 13 ft. They are made of rubberised fabric and have a long fin of some 4 to 5 ft. at the base.

The leaflet-carrying box is slung underneath, and consists of a small cardboard box in cube form with an 8½ in. side, in the centre compartment of which is a simple clockwork mechanism. Around this are four compartments (see Figure 22), containing bundles of leaflets which are held in position by wire bands until the moment of release.

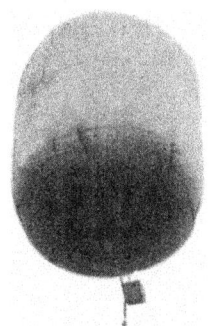

FIGURE 21

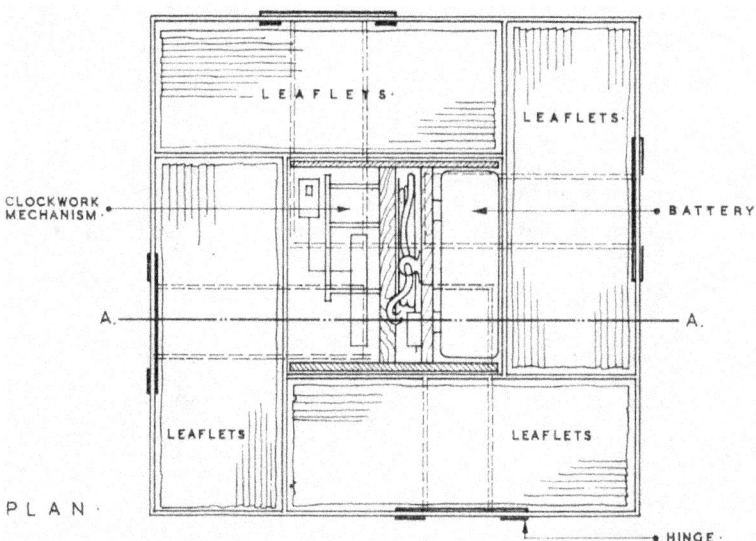

FIGURE 22

The clockwork mechanism drives two pulleys, round one of which is wound a thin wire and round the other a silk cord. The thin wire unwinds off the pulley under the impulse of the clockwork and lets fall the wire bands clear of the bottom of the box, thereby releasing the leaflets. In a small compartment adjoining the clockwork a dry cell is held between two spring clips. Leads from this cell are carried into a small bag of flash powder, and contacts on the clockwork side are arranged to give a delayed action.

When the box is found unopened on the ground, it is only necessary to reverse the battery end for end in the clips to prevent this powder being fired. Injuries have been caused in certain cases through the omission to take this precaution.

16. Leaflet-carrying Parachutes.

Prior to the use of balloons for this purpose, the Germans dropped leaflets by means of parachutes, the leaflets being carried in bundles and secured by a simple wire device which was broken open by a small explosive charge. It is possible this practice may be resumed.

17. Man-carrying Parachutes.

German man-carrying parachutes are of two types :—

(*a*) A seat type harness where the wearer sits on the parachute pack.

(*b*) A pack type which is carried on the wearer's back.

The parachutes have white canopies, usually of artificial silk, and are opened by pulling a rip cord releasing a pilot parachute, which in turn opens the main one. The pilot parachute is in eight segments, alternate segments being opened by four wire or strip metal springs. The length of seam is 16 in. ; top width of segment approximately 3 in. and bottom width about $12\frac{1}{2}$ in.

The main parachute is in twenty-four segments. The length of seam is 10 ft. 6 in. to 10 ft. 9 in. ; width of segment at top, 3 in., and at bottom, 2 ft. 11 in. to 3 ft. 2 in.

In the seat type, the harness rigging lines are retained in six hanks by canvas loops, and in the pack type by five canvas loops.

The following markings have been found on German Emergency Parachutes :—

(*a*) On the underside of seat type :

Sitzfallschirm	(Seat-type parachute)	
Baumuster	(Pattern)	3OIS24BSA
Werknummer	(Works No.)	2000480
Gewicht	(Weight)	9.5 kg.
Tag der Herstellung	(Date of Manufacture)	1 Feb. 1939
Anforderungszeichen	(Reference No.)	F L 30201
Hersteller	(Maker)	AUTOFLUG, Berlin.

(*b*) On the belt clasp of pack type :

AUSLOSEN

DREHEN DANN DRUCKEN. (To open, turn and then push.)

An artificial silk parachute of similar dimensions has been reported which has cords dyed sepia and the canopy camouflaged in an all-over pattern of emerald green, gold and olive green.

18. British Practice Bombs.

The overall length, including fins, is 16 in., and the fins are 3 in. long. The bomb is tapered, has a maximum diameter of 3 in. and has usually a lug about 5 in. from the nose. The bomb weighs 9¼ lb.

When uncharged the bomb is painted white, without markings. **If charged, it is painted white with two ¼ in. green bands ½ in. apart round the centre of the tail unit.**

19. British Smoke Floats.

The British smoke float has an overall length of 22 in. and is 5¾ in. in diameter. It weighs about 10 lb. when complete:

The cases are painted green with the following markings stencilled in black lettering :—

Mark ; date of filling ; filling contractors' initials or trade-mark ; a ½ in. red band 1 in. from the nose.

———

In addition to the objects enumerated above, unexploded anti-aircraft shells as well as certain British experimental devices are likely to be found, the characteristics of which have been described in circulars addressed to the Police and Civil Defence Authorities, but which cannot conveniently be included in the present handbook.

NOTES.

CONFIDENTIAL

MINISTRY OF HOME SECURITY

OBJECTS DROPPED FROM THE AIR

ADDENDUM No. 1

Since the preparation of the above-mentioned Handbook, the objects described below have either been brought into use—or in the case of the last item, reported frequently enough to warrant a description being circulated.

---

1. **German H.E. Weapons.**
    Additional items:
    (*a*) Type " ' G ' Mine."
    (*b*) Illustration of German anti-personnel bomb.
2. **Incendiary Bomb Containers.**
    Types e (i) and e (ii). (*See p.* 10 *of Handbook.*)
3. **Meteorological Balloons.**
    Recent modifications. (*See p.* 16 *of Handbook.*)
4. **British Trench-Mortar Bombs.**
    Additional category No. 20.

Type ' G ' Mine.

A recent addition to the range of German H.E. weapons is a new type of mine which the three Services have agreed to be known as the ' G ' type mine. (*See figure* 23.)

It has no parachute, but on to the tail unit cover are fitted tail rings and fins of brown bakelised material painted light blue, which easily break off on impact. (*See figure* 24.)

General dimensions* are as follows :—

Length overall, 6 ft. 4 in. (omitting the tail fins).

Diameter of body, 2 ft. 2 in.

Total weight about 2,160 lb.

The weapon is a mine of the magnetic type and is usually painted light blue. Any metal object, e.g. a spade in the immediate vicinity, might cause detonation.

The unexploded ' G ' mine is likely to be buried and cannot be identified from its hole of entry, which will be the same as that of a large bomb. Fragments of bakelite will, however, generally indicate its presence, although fins of this material have been observed on a very few German bombs, and the tail cover dome, which is of unusual shape, may be found broken off by impact.

The tail fin assembly carries the following markings in red letters 2 cm. high printed on paper labels :—

(*a*) On the collar of the fins : " *Hier nicht anheben* " (Do not lift here).

(*b*) On one or more fins: "*Vorsicht—Leicht verletzbar*"(With care—fragile).

The nose of one such mine was inscribed " Zu verbrauchen bis März 1942 Bk. 1.4.41. 1609." (To be used before March, 1942. Manufactured 1.4.41.)

Fig. 23.
TYPE " G " MINE.

In the light of this information the second paragraph on p. 8 of the original handbook should be amended as follows :—

Clause (*a*) should now read " Bombs are fitted with fins ; parachute mines are not."

Clause (*b*) should be deleted, and clauses (*c*) *and* (*d*) now become (*b*) *and* (*c*) respectively.

---

*N.B.—These may be compared with the ' C ' and ' D ' type mines which are now respectively established as 8 ft. 8 in. and 5 ft. 8 in. long without the tail bowl.

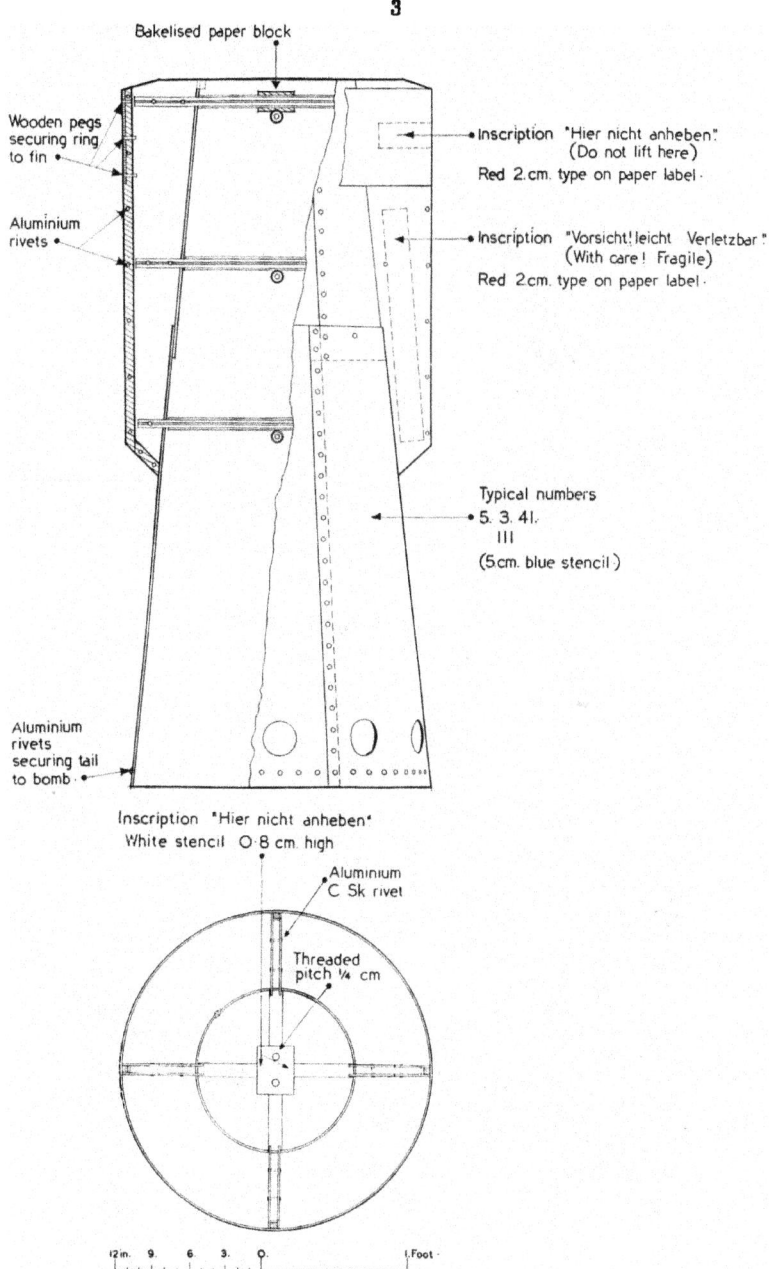

Fig. 24.
TYPE "G" MINE TAIL UNIT.

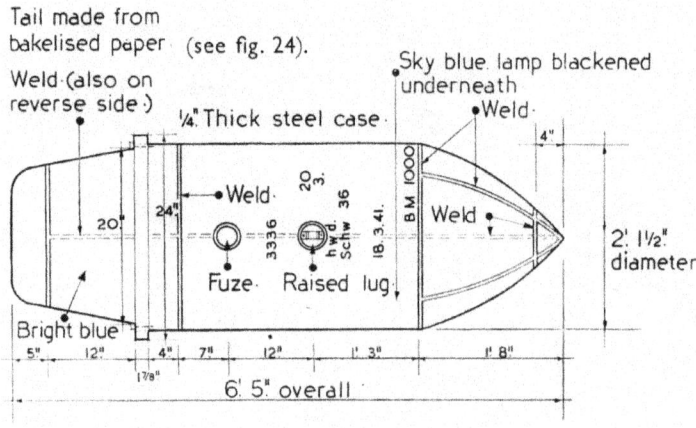

Fig. 25.
GERMAN MINE, TYPE "G."

German Anti-Personnel Bombs.

Figure 26 shows in outline and gives the principal dimensions of the German 10 kg. Anti-Personnel Bomb. This is on a scale twice as large as that of the H.E. bombs illustrated in *Figure* 1 of the Handbook. (*N.B.— Specimens have now been found to weigh, with fuse, 12 kg.*)

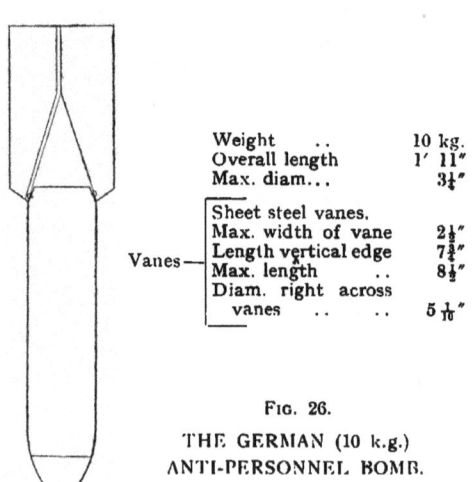

Weight	..	10 kg.
Overall length		1' 11"
Max. diam...		3¼"
Sheet steel vanes.		
Max. width of vane		2½"
Vanes — Length vertical edge		7¾"
Max. length	..	8½"
Diam. right across vanes	.. ..	5 1/10"

Fig. 26.
THE GERMAN (10 k.g.) ANTI-PERSONNEL BOMB.

Incendiary Bomb Containers.

A fifth type of German incendiary bomb container has now been brought into use. It has been found in two sizes but the general design is the same in both and consists of a cylinder divided into compartments. (*See Figs.* 12c. *and* 12d.) To conform with the notation used in the Handbook these may conveniently be referred to as types *e* (*i*) and *e* (*ii*).

Type *e* (*i*), the larger pattern, is about 2 ft. 2 in. in diameter, 10 ft. 3 in. long and has six compartments, the whole containing 702 1-kg. incendiary bombs. It weighs 205 kg. (450 lb.) empty and 900 kg. (1,980 lb.) full.

Type *e* (*ii*) is 1 ft. 8 in. in diameter, 7 ft. 9 in. long and is divided into four compartments, the total content being 360 bombs. It is painted black and weighs 75 kg. (166 lb.) empty and 435 kg. (960 lb.) full.

The contents of each compartment are released by means of trap-doors operated from an axial spindle, the release mechanism being electrically controlled in type *e* (*i*) and by cables in type *e* (*ii*).

The whole container is carried externally in the aircraft, and has presumably been designed to increase the incendiary load capacity of existing types.

The container is made of sheet steel $\frac{1}{16}$ in. thick and has a blunt nose with the tail portion tapered like that of a bomb.

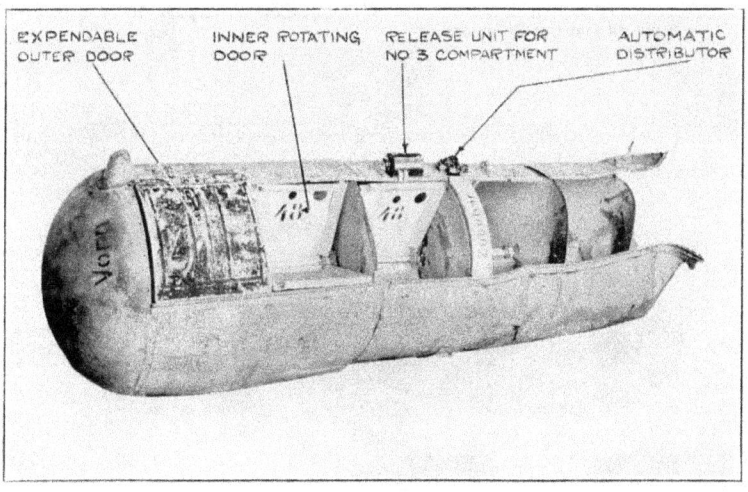

Fig. 12c.

INCENDIARY BOMB CONTAINER

Type *e* (*i*).

The following inscriptions have been reported on one such container examined in this country :—

On the top towards one end :—

Beladezahl (Charge), 700±5.

Leergewicht (Weight empty), 205 kg.

Gesamtgewicht (Total weight), 900 kg.

On the cover of the container over the narrow central compartment : *Zubëhor* (Accessories).

At one end of each releasing unit is a thumb lever, and on the side is fixed a small metal plate with this inscription :—

Schübvorgang : Knopf eindrücken, Hebel gleichzeitig schieben. Offnungs vorgang : Knopf 2 mal eindrücken. (To shut : Press the button, at the same time slide the handle. To Open : Press the button twice.)

At the other end of the releasing unit there is a smaller plate with the following inscription :—

Bauart (Construction) e k v.

Sach Nr. (Item No.) 18-903.03.

Werk Nr. (Job. No.) 1900124.

Anforderz. Fl. (Reference No.) 50683.

Hersteller (Maker) e k v.

N.B.—It is now known that the type '*a*' containers (*c.f. page* 10 *of Handbook*) hold 36 and not 24 bombs.

Fig. 12D.

INCENDIARY BOMB CONTAINER
Type *e* (*ii*).

Meteorological Balloons.

The smaller balloons described in *Section* 14 of the Handbook sometimes carry a small Chinese lantern at the end of the tail. Typical meteorographs carried by the larger balloons are illustrated in *Figures* 27 *and* 28, the former showing a British instrument with parachute as it would be found after falling.

Of the instruments shown in *Figure* 28 the two in the middle are British while those on the outside are German. The outer casings, from left to right, are made of celluloid, bakelised cardboard, aluminium and bakelised cardboard respectively. In all these instruments the meteorological elements are surrounded by aluminium shields.

It has been found that the Germans are now using balloons of French manufacture, similar in construction to the British type. The distinguishing features mentioned in the second paragraph of *Section* 14 may, therefore, not always be present.

Fig. 27.
METEOROLOGICAL BALLOON

Fig. 28.
TYPICAL METEOROGRAPHS.

British Trench-Mortar Bomb.

The type of British trench-mortar bomb shown in *Figures* 29 *and* 30 is sometimes mistaken for a German incendiary bomb. It has a cylindrical body 2 in. in diameter and $5\frac{1}{2}$ in. long with a tail fuse unit $3\frac{1}{2}$ in. long terminating in a milled screw cover about $\frac{3}{4}$ in. in diameter. There are six vanes with three holes in the stem between each vane; the blunt nose of the bomb has three rivet heads in the face and typical markings are shown in the accompanying Figures.

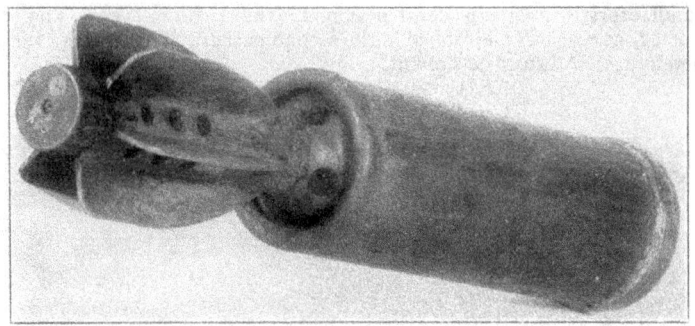

FIG. 29.
TRENCH MORTAR BOMB.

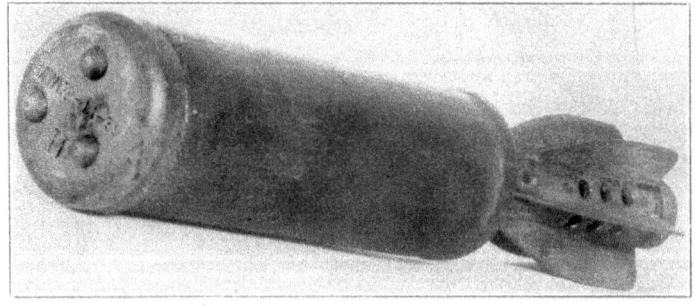

FIG. 30.
TRENCH MORTAR BOMB.

www.ingramcontent.com/pod-product-compliance
Lightning Source LLC
Chambersburg PA
CBHW070455050426
42450CB00012B/3280